AMAZING STRUCTURES
TUNNELS

by Rebecca Pettiford

Pogo Books let children practice reading informational text while introducing them to nonfiction features such as headings, labels, sidebars, maps, and diagrams, as well as a table of contents, glossary, and index.

Carefully leveled text with a strong photo match offers early fluent readers the support they need to succeed.

Before Reading

"Walk" through the book and point out the various nonfiction features. Ask the student what purpose each feature serves.

Look at the glossary together. Read and discuss the words.

Read the Book

Have the child read the book independently.

Invite him or her to list questions that arise from reading.

After Reading

Discuss the child's questions. Talk about how he or she might find answers to those questions.

Prompt the child to think more. Ask: Is there a tunnel where you live that you go through often? What is the longest tunnel you've even been in?

Pogo Books are published by Jump!
475 North Frontage Road
Suite 200
Mankato, MN 56003
www.jumplibrary.com

Copyright © 2018 Jump!
International copyright reserved in all countries.
No part of this book may be reproduced in any form
without written permission from the publisher.

Library of Congress Cataloging-in-Publication Data

Names and Descriptions
Title: Tunnels / by Rebecca Pettiford.
Description: Pogo books edition.
Minneapolis, MN:
Jump!, Inc., [2018] | Series: Engineering wonders
Includes bibliographical references and index.
Identifiers: LCCN 2017006637 (print)
LCCN 2017023116 (ebook)
ISBN 9781620312124
Subjects: Tunnels—Juvenile literature.
Classification: LCC TA807 (ebook)
LCC TA807 .P48 2018 (print)

Editor: Jenna Trnka
Book Designer: Molly Ballanger
Photo Researcher: Molly Ballanger

Photo credits: All photographs by Shutterstock.com
except: AP Images, 16-17; Corbis, 14-15, 18-19;
iStock, 8, 10; Dreamstime, 1, 11; Science Source,
3; Superstock, 4-5, 6-7; Thinkstock, 9, 12-13, 22.

Printed in the United States of America at
Corporate Graphics in North Mankato, Minnesota.

TABLE OF CONTENTS

CHAPTER 1

WHAT IS A TUNNEL?

What's that up ahead? A **tunnel**!

A tunnel is a passage that goes through or under roads, mountains, rivers, and oceans.

Early Greeks and Romans built **mines** to dig up gold. They also built tunnels called **aqueducts**. These tunnels carried fresh water to cities.

The invention of trains
and cars led to more
tunnels being built.
Powerful new tools made
it possible to build bigger
and longer tunnels.

How do people build
tunnels? Let's take a look.

CHAPTER 2

BUILDING TUNNELS

Tunnels need to be safe. Planning is important.

Engineers look at the soil or rock to learn what material they will be working with.

Once they make a plan, construction can begin.

Workers need to do three things to build a safe tunnel.

First, they need to use tools that will work best for the job.

Second, they must control the rock or soil as they dig.

Third, they must put in a strong **lining**. It helps support the weight of the material above. It makes the tunnel safe.

DID YOU KNOW?

Digging a tunnel is dangerous work. The tunnel could cave in and hurt workers. The air may not be safe to breathe.

lining ······▶

◀······

Tunnels can make travel safer.

Boats often face bad weather. An **underwater tunnel** like the Channel Tunnel is a solution.

WHERE IS IT?

The Channel Tunnel connects England and France. The part that is underwater is 23 miles (37 kilometers) long.

ENGLAND

FRANCE

●━━● = Channel Tunnel

CHAPTER 3

TYPES OF TUNNELS

There are several types of tunnels. Let's look at a few.

rock tunnel

◄ · · · · · ·

To build **rock tunnels**, workers use a **boring machine**. It drills large holes into the earth.

It can drill both up and down. This makes it useful for digging into mountains. Workers also use it to dig other types of tunnels.

Subways use **soft ground tunnels**. Workers build them in clay, sand, or mud.

They use a steel **tunnel shield** to dig a hole. It holds the soil up while workers remove waste. Then they put in a lining. When they are done, they push the shield forward.

DID YOU KNOW?

The Laerdal Tunnel in Norway is the longest road tunnel in the world. It is more than 15 miles (24 kilometers) long. Drivers spend about 20 minutes traveling through the inside of a mountain!

tunnel shield

clay

tunnel piece

seal

To build underwater tunnels,
workers must hold the water back.

To do this, they use pre-made
tunnel pieces. Each piece
is sealed to keep out water.
They fit the pieces into place.
Then they remove the seals.

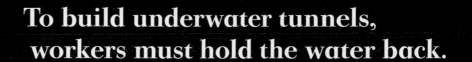

DID YOU KNOW?

The Bund Sightseeing Tunnel
is an underwater tunnel
in China. Colorful visual
effects play as people
go through it.

Now that you know about tunnels, are you ready to go through one?

It will be dark, but don't worry. Many people worked hard to make it safe.

ACTIVITIES & TOOLS

EXPLORE A TUNNEL

In this activity, you will use the Internet to learn more about a tunnel. If you need help using the Internet, ask an adult.

Find out if there is a tunnel in your town. If not, what is a famous tunnel in your state? You may decide to learn more about a tunnel you saw in this book. Learn everything you can about your tunnel. Answer the following questions:

❶ **What is your tunnel called and where is it located?**

❷ **What kind of tunnel is it? Does it run through rock, soft ground, or underwater?**

❸ **When was it built?**

❹ **How long is it?**

❺ **What problems, if any, did workers face during its construction?**

❻ **Is there anything special or unusual about the tunnel?**

GLOSSARY

aqueducts: Human-made channels for transporting water.

boring machine: A drilling machine used to dig out tunnels.

engineers: People who plan and build tunnels and other structures.

lining: A support structure, usually made of steel, that makes a tunnel secure.

mines: Areas where earth is dug up to remove minerals (such as coal) and metals (such as gold); many mines are underground.

rock tunnels: Tunnels that go through rock or mountains.

soft ground tunnels: Tunnels that are built in clay, sand, or mud.

tunnel: A passage through a roadway, mountain, or under the water.

tunnel shield: A steel structure workers use for protection when they dig tunnels through soft soil.

underwater tunnels: Tunnels that go under a river or ocean.

INDEX

TO LEARN MORE

Learning more is as easy as 1, 2, 3.

1) **Go to www.factsurfer.com**

2) **Enter "tunnels" into the search box.**

3) **Click the "Surf" to see a list of websites.**

With factsurfer, finding more information is just a click away.